Where Is Melina?

Melanie Cameron
Morgan Cameron
Doreen Cameron
R. Travis Cameron, Photographer

Dedication

**This book is dedicated to Melina who is a
master at hiding!**

Acknowledgements
Thanks to Don, Caleb, Doreen, Larissa, and
June for seeking Melina as she hid all around
the house and yard.

This is Melina. She is three years old. Melina likes to laugh and play.

Melina has two older sisters. She likes to hide from them. See if you can find Melina in some of her favorite hiding spots.

Melina's mom just did the laundry. Can you see Melina?

There's Melina! She is hiding underneath all those clothes!

Melina and her sisters have lots of stuffed animals. Can you see Melina?

There's Melina! She is snuggling with her stuffed bear.

Melina and her sisters have a big doll house. Can you see Melina?

There's Melina! Her feet are hanging out of the window.

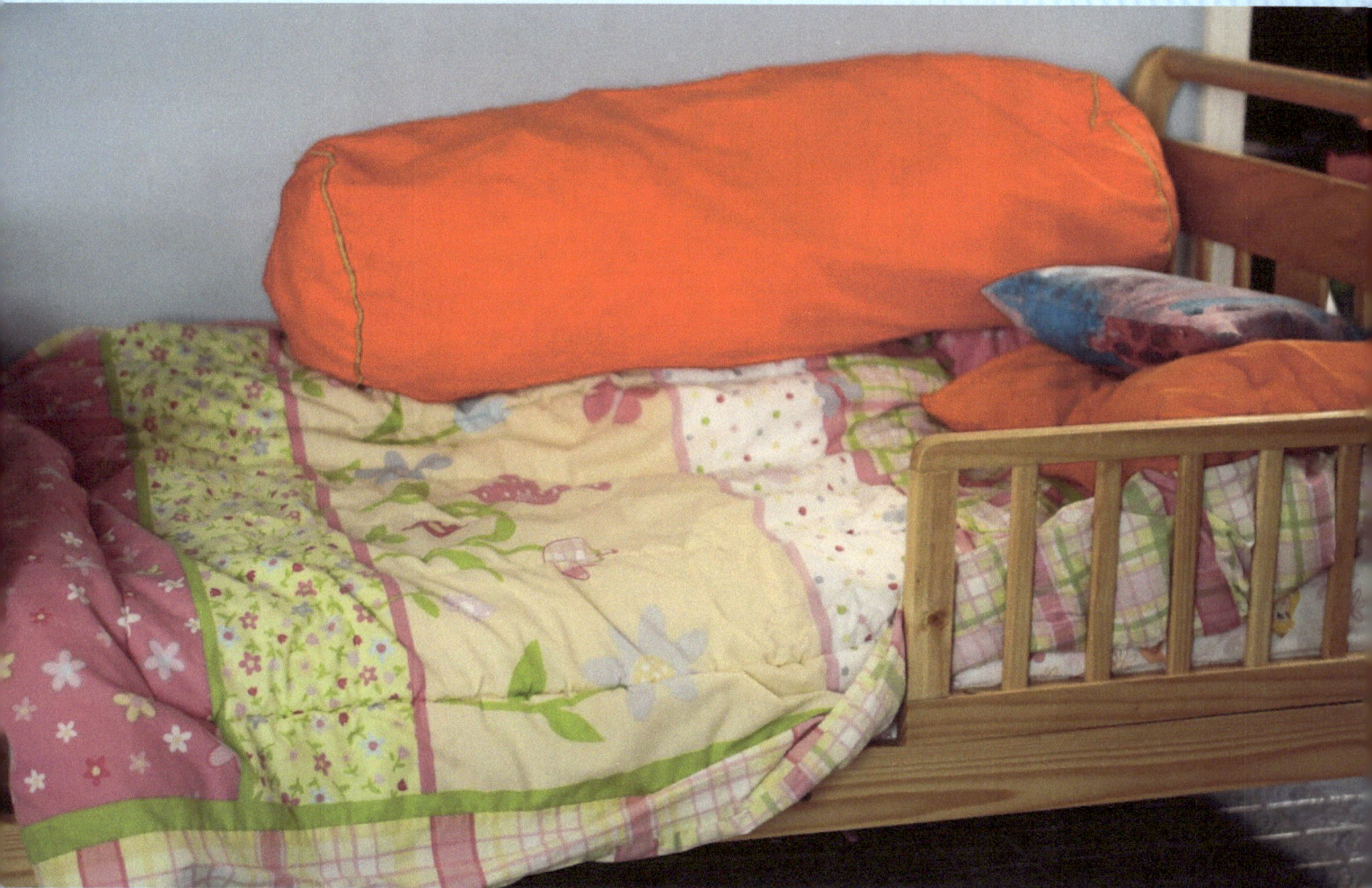

This is Melina's bed. She pulled her quilt up and placed her pillows nicely before she went to play. Can you see Melina?

There's Melina! She was hiding underneath her orange body pillow!

This is the slide that Melina and her sisters like to play on. Can you see Melina?

There's Melina! She was hiding underneath the slide. It is like her own little playhouse.

Melina's mommy went grocery shopping. It's time to put away the food. Can you see Melina?

There's Melina! How did she get inside that shopping bag?

Melina and her sisters helped to fold and put away the towels. Can you see Melina?

There's Melina! How did she get behind all those towels?

Mom made bread bowls and soup for dinner. Let's eat! Can you see Melina?

There's Melina! Now we can all sit down to eat.

This is where mommy stores all her pots and pans. Can you see Melina?

There's Melina! She's not old enough to cook, yet.

Daddy has been working in his office. Can you see Melina?

There's Melina! She was sitting in daddy's chair.

Melina and her sisters were working in the garden. Can you see Melina?

There's Melina! She was hiding in the bushes by the driveway.

There is a little cave in Melina's back yard. She and her sisters are afraid of the spiders that are sometimes in the cave. Can you see Melina?

There's Melina! She didn't see any spiders in the cave today.

Grandma and Grandpa have a big coffee table. Can you see Melina?

There's Melina! I wonder what surprises she has hidden under there.

Grandma and Grandpa have a comfortable couch. Can you see Melina?

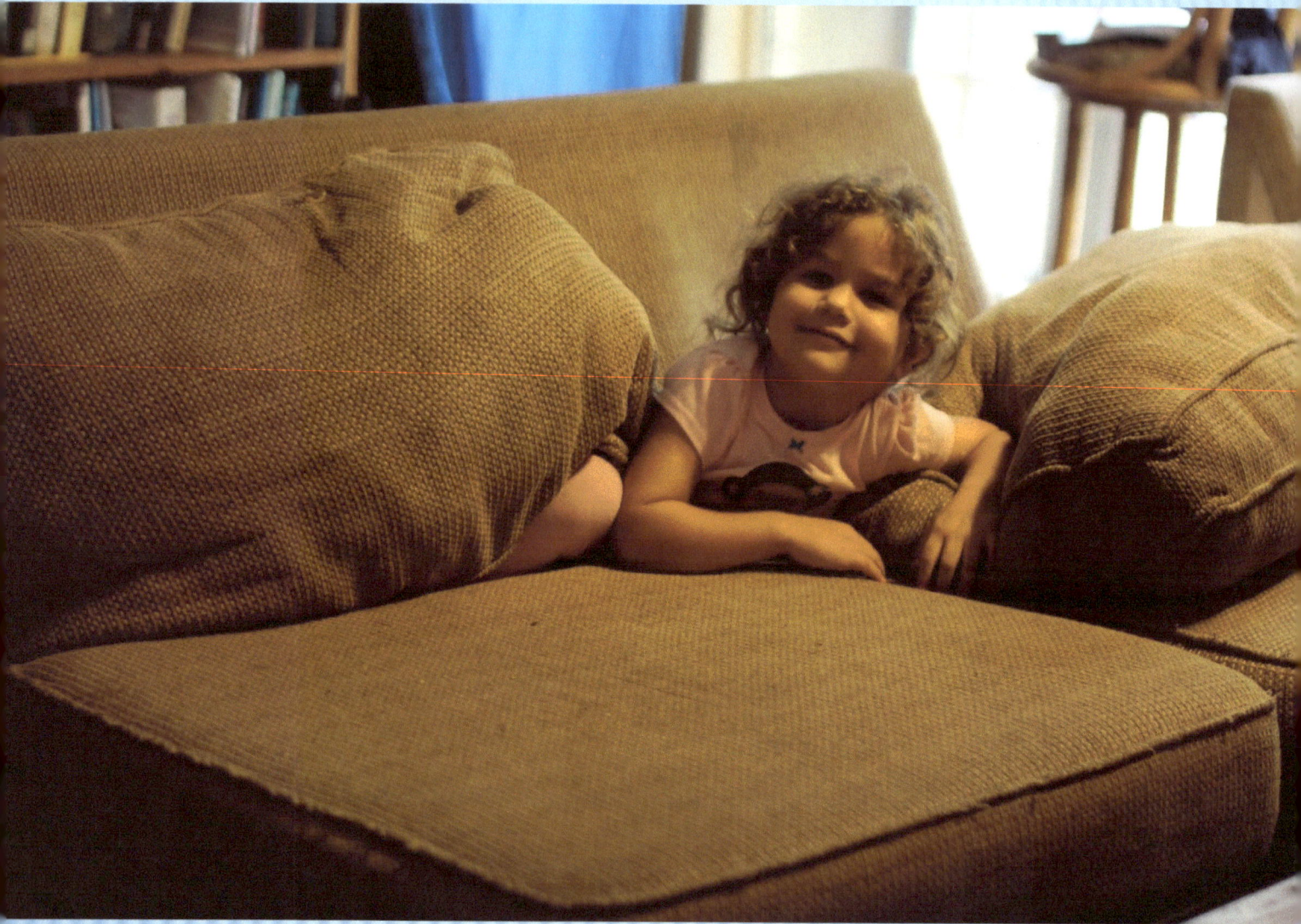

There's Melina! You better move before
Uncle Caleb and Aunty Morgan come and
sit on you.

Melina has had a busy day. Now it's time for her bath. Can you see Melina?

**There's Melina! All covered with
bubbles!**

Thanks for playing hide and seek with Melina today. Come back tomorrow and we can jump into some more fun!

Melanie is Melina's grandma. She came up with the idea of doing this book one day when Melina kept hiding in the laundry basket and the stuffed animal bucket. She also put the book together.

Morgan is Melina's aunty. She is the one who started hiding Melina. She also came up with all of the fun hiding spots for Melina.

Travis and Doreen are Melina's parents. Travis took most of the pictures for this book. Doreen assisted with all aspects of this project.